The British postal service is one of the oldest in the world and every working day it handles millions of letters, packets and parcels. Collections are made from postboxes and post offices and delivered to over 22 million addresses. This book with colour photographs, most of which were specially taken for the book, explains in simple language how the system works and looks behind the scenes at the working lives of postmen and postwomen.

Acknowledgments
The author and publishers would like to thank the following for their assistance during the preparation of this book: Post Office staff at Loughborough, Leicester, Derby and Peterborough sorting offices; East Midlands airport; and the photographic library at Post Office Headquarters for the photographs on pages 8, 9, 11 (top), 26, 27, 28, 31 (bottom), 32, 33, 36, 37 and back endpaper.

First Edition

© LADYBIRD BOOKS LTD MCMLXXXIII

People who help us

THE POSTAL SERVICE

written by RON EDWARDS

photographs by TIM CLARK

Ladybird Books Loughborough

When you post a letter do you ever wonder what will happen to it before a postman or postwoman delivers it through someone's letter-box?

A postman delivers the mail

When you post a letter, the metal or plastic plate on the front of the postbox will tell you what time the postman will next come and empty the box

First of all a postman will come in a van to collect all the letters from the *postbox*.

People have to hand parcels, registered letters and other special kinds of *mail* over the counter at a *post office*.

Parcels or packets can be weighed on the scales at the post office and this will tell you how much you must pay to send them

The van takes the letters from the postbox to the local sorting office.

Bags of mail and large parcels are loaded into a mail van

Then all the mail, letters, packets and parcels are put into bags and sealed.

The bags are loaded in a big van which will take them to the post office in the nearest large town. Larger post offices have big *sorting offices*.

The van carrying the mailbags arrives at the *loading bay*. The bags are hooked on to a *chain conveyor* which carries them up to the sorting office.

In the sorting office the hooks which are holding the bags, open at *drop-off* points.

Mailbags are hooked on to the chain conveyor

The bags drop on to chutes and slide down to benches where postmen and postwomen separate the packets and very large envelopes from the rest of the mail.

In the most modern *mechanised* sorting offices the bags are emptied into a *segregator*. It *automatically* separates packets and very large envelopes from the rest.

Mail travels up a moving belt into the segregator drum

Inside the segregator is a large drum which revolves. The sides of the drum are hinged flaps which allow the ordinary letters to slip through the slots in between the flaps.

Top: *Inside the segregator. The thick envelopes and packets pass onto a conveyor belt which takes them to benches where they are sorted by hand*

The ordinary envelopes are sorted by size and shape into three groups by the segregator

11

When you have addressed a letter and put on the *postcode* you must stick on a stamp. If you want it to go quickly you use a *First Class* stamp. Then your letter should arrive the next working day, if you post it early enough. *Second Class* mail takes longer.

The piles of first or second class mail are taken from the ALF when they have been faced, cancelled and postmarked

The ordinary sized letters from the segregator now go into ALF, the *Automatic Letter Facer*. It turns all the letters round so that the stamps are in the correct position in the top right-hand corner. This is called *facing*.

ALF separates the letters into first and second class mail and *cancels* the stamp on each one.

ALF also prints the *postmark* on the envelope. This shows at which post office the letter was sorted and on what date.

Next, the letters have to be *coded* ready for sorting. At the coding desk an operator sits at a keyboard like a typewriter.

An operator types the postcode

As soon as a letter is coded it travels along a conveyor belt to the pre-sorter (see page 17)

Every time the operator presses a pedal, a letter moves in front of him or her and stops while the postcode is typed. Some operators can code more than 3,000 letters an hour.

The postcode is the mixture of letters and figures at the bottom of the address.

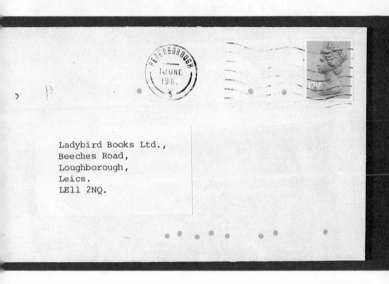

Ladybird Books Ltd.,
Beeches Road,
Loughborough,
Leics.
LE11 2NQ.

The top row of dots means Ladybird Books *in* Beeches Road. *The bottom row means* Loughborough *in* Leicestershire

When the operator types the postcode, the machine prints pale blue dots on the top and bottom of the envelope. The bottom row stands for the town and district. The top row stands for the sector and street. The dots are *phosphor dots* which glow when a special light shines on them.

When the mail reaches the sorting office nearest its destination it is sorted again. If it is machine-sorted the top row of dots will be used.

The pre-sorter 'reads' the bottom row of dots and sorts out the mail to give priority to those letters with furthest to travel

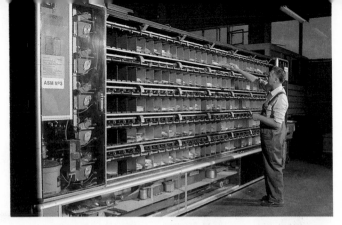

Above and below: *The ASM, with the aid of ultra-violet light, 'reads' the blue dots. It sorts the mail into 138 main destinations at 16,000 letters per hour*

The coded letters are now fed into the *Automatic Letter Sorting Machine* (ASM).

The ASM can 'read' the shining dots. The sorting office from which the letter is being sent will only read the bottom row.

The control panel of the ASM

The letter in the picture on page 16 will end up with all the others going to that district. At the local mechanical sorting office another ASM will read the top row.

Letters for a particular city, town or large area are kept together and labelled

In smaller sorting offices all the sorting is still done by hand. First the mail is segregated.

Next, the letters are taken to *sorting frames*. The *primary sorters* sort the mail which has been collected in the town, into counties and other large areas. Each *pigeon hole* has a label. The outgoing mail will be sent all over the country and to other parts of the world.

Primary sorting is into *roads*. Everywhere north of the sorting office is, for example, called the *north road*. How the postmen name their 'roads' depends where the sorting office is in the country.

Primary sorting

Sorting packets and smaller parcels into drop-bags

Even in a modern sorting office with machines, packets and large envelopes have to be sorted and cancelled by hand.

They are sorted into *drop-bags* instead of pigeon holes.

Secondary sorters will sort the *roads* from the primary sorting, into towns and districts.

Local or *incoming* mail which has been sent from other sorting offices, is sorted ready for delivery. The postmen and postwomen will sort the mail into the correct order for the houses on their rounds.

Secondary sorting by the postman

The sorted parcels drop down the chute and are put into a wooden container called a MATE (Mail All-purpose Trailer Equipment)

Parcels are not dealt with in ordinary sorting offices. They are put into special wooden containers and taken to the nearest *Parcels Concentration Office* (PCO) to be sorted.

The operator in the control room at the PCO can see, on small TV screens, when chutes are full or blocked

In charge of every large postal area is a *Postmaster*. Departments like the sorting office will have *postal executives* in charge. All the sorting, collection and deliveries are done by postmen or postwomen.

A postman begins his deliveries. In towns, or in areas with a lot of mail, the postman may use a trolley to carry his mail

When all the outgoing mail has been sorted it is put into bags and sent down the chute to the loading bay. There it is put into vans. The vans will take the mail to a railway station, a port or an airport. Most mail goes by train and many large sorting offices have a tunnel between them and their local railway station.

At this sorting office, a tunnel goes from the sorting office down to the railway platform where the mail is loaded on the train. A small tractor pulls a line of trailers loaded with mailbags

The control room operator watches the progress of the Post Office's underground railway system

In London, the Post Office has its own underground railway. It carries mail between six sorting offices and two main railway stations.

Left: *The railway collects mailbags from the sorting offices*
Above: *Royal Mail trains being loaded at Euston station in London. These trains will travel through the night*

27

Travelling Post Offices (TPOs) are railway carriages fitted out as mobile sorting offices. Postmen sort the mail while the train travels to its destination. The Post Office pays British Rail for these TPO vehicles and to run a rail service at times which suit the postal service

Mail being unloaded from a plane at East Midlands airport

More and more *inland mail* is carried between big towns by air.

The bags are loaded into a Royal Mail van

Royal Mail

Links by air and rail from East Midlands

——— air

+++++++ rail

Inverness
Aberdeen
Glasgow
Edinburgh
Newcastle
York
Liverpool
Sheffield
Crewe
Lincoln
East Midlands Airport
Derby
Nottingham
Birmingham
Leicester
Norwich
Peterborough
Gloucester
Stansted
Bristol
London
Southend
Southampton
Gatwick
Newquay
Exeter

All letters and postcards to Europe go by air, too. If you want to send an *airmail* letter to any other country you can use a special envelope or an *airletter*. You may also stick an airmail label on an ordinary envelope.

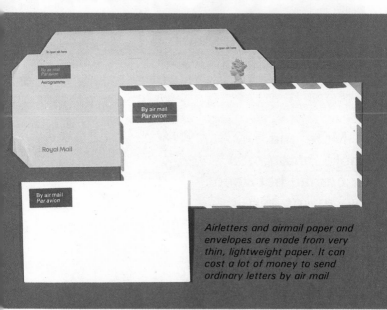

Airletters and airmail paper and envelopes are made from very thin, lightweight paper. It can cost a lot of money to send ordinary letters by air mail

After all the sorting is finished, the letters are ready for delivery. Each postman or postwoman has to deliver letters in a particular area called a *walk*.

It is still called a walk if the postman goes by bicycle. In country districts postmen deliver letters and parcels by bicycle or van.

Sometimes a *postbus* is used and passengers travel on it, too.

A postbus in a Welsh town

Boats are used to deliver mail to ships in ports and to people who live on islands.

There are many special mail services offered by the Post Office. If you need proof that a letter has been

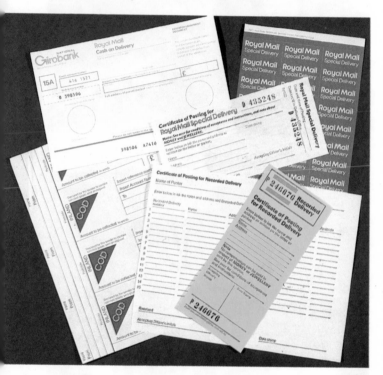

Forms and labels for different kinds of special delivery

delivered you can use *Recorded Delivery*. You pay extra and fill in a form. A special label is stuck on the envelope.

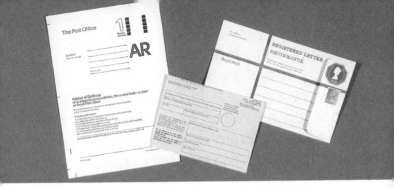

If you put a stamp on an *Advice of Delivery card*, the card will be sent to you when your letter is delivered.

To send cash, or something else which is valuable, you should use a *Registered Letter Envelope* and pay an extra fee. If the packet is lost you will get back a sum of money.

Some of the other services provided by the Post Office

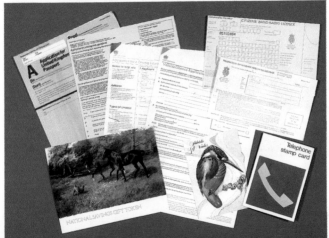

If you wish mail to be delivered very quickly there are several *Express Delivery* services. In London and some other large towns, *Expresspost* letters are collected and delivered door-to-door by motorcycle messengers.

An Expresspost motorcyclist

Business people often use *Datapost* to send important papers. The papers are collected and delivered door-to-door overnight. *Swiftair* is an express delivery service to places overseas.

A postman in New York, USA, delivers a Datapost package

There is free postage for blind people. People use it to post *talking books* and things written in *Braille*. You can also send a harness for a guide dog free of charge.

Business people often want customers to be able to write to them free of postage. They send *Freepost* or *Business Reply* envelopes. When they are posted back they go to a special sorting bench. A machine counts them and the Post Office sends the business a bill.

Businesses which send out a great deal of mail can have *franking machines*. They print stamps on envelopes. People who have them pay a special fee to the Post Office.

Each envelope is weighed and the franking machine prints the correct amount in the place of a stamp, plus a postmark. Different businesses can use different words or pictures as part of their cancellation mark. At Ladybird Books it is a picture of a ladybird

Some businesses with lots of
incoming mail prefer not to wait for
the usual deliveries. Instead they have

Mail for Ladybird Books is collected from the local sorting office

a private bag or box at the local post
office. Staff go to collect the mail.

The heavier a letter is, the more it will cost. It also costs more to send one overseas.

A stamp vending machine which provides books of stamps

Buying stamps at a post office counter

You buy postage stamps at a post office. They can be bought singly or in books. If the post office is closed you may find a *stamp vending machine* outside.

Stamps are issued to commemorate special occasions. They are often very beautiful and interesting. That is why many people collect stamps as a hobby.

The world's first adhesive *postage stamp was the* Penny Black. *It was issued in 1840*

A selection of commemorative stamps

Behind the counter at a head post-office

There are three kinds of post office.
As well as the larger head post
offices there are *salaried sub-post
offices* and *agency sub-post offices*.
The Post Office owns the buildings of
the head and salaried sub-post
offices.

A sub-post office

The agency sub-post office is usually a shop. The Post Office pays the shopkeepers who act as sub-postmasters. The more business they do the more they are paid.

This post office is part of a shop

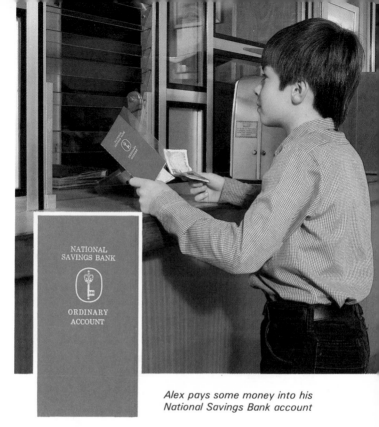

Alex pays some money into his National Savings Bank account

You can do much more than buy stamps and post letters at a post office. If you are over seven years old you can put money into the *National Savings Bank* and get it out. If you are younger, grown-ups can put money in for you but you cannot take it out until you are seven.

Getting a pension from the post office

People go to a post office to draw their *pensions*. Parents go to get *family allowances*. Unemployed people get their benefit from it.

All the hundreds of forms and leaflets needed by a post office are stored ready for use

All kinds of *licences* are bought at the post office. You need a licence if you keep a dog.

If you have a radio or television set you must buy a licence at a post office.

DOG LICENCE (£0·37½)
(NOT TRANSFERABLE) **WK** 240400

Full Christian Names

and Surname
(ON BLOCK LETTERS)
Full Postal Address

is hereby authorised to keep **ONE DOG** in Great Britain, from the *date hereof* until and including the *last day of** _____ *next following;* the sum of THIRTY-SEVEN and a HALF PENCE having been paid for this Licence.

Granted at _____ hours _____ minutes _____ m. o'clock at the place and on the date indicated in the issuing office stamp.

by _____

NOTICE.—Any permanent change of address should be notified to the appropriate District or Island Council.

Penalty for refusing to show this Licence to any duly authorised Officer, or Police Constable, or for keeping a dog above 6 months old without Licence, £10

*Insert month preceding the month of next issue of this Licence.   **SEE NOTES OVERLEAF**

Small sums of money may be sent by post using *postal orders*. You pay a fee when you buy one.

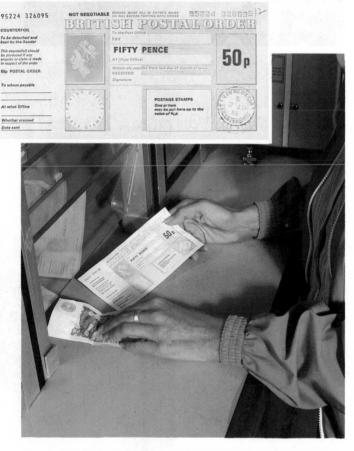

If you can't write a cheque, postal orders are the safest way to send money through the post

If you are over fifteen you can join the *National Girobank*. You get a book of cheques and it works just like an ordinary bank but everything is done at a post office.

These are some of the many services offered by the Post Office.

Each day about 35 million letters and other items are delivered to over 22 million postal addresses. The use of machinery is helping to speed up the service and make it more efficient.

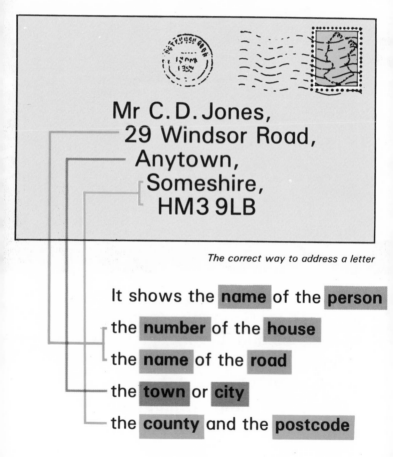

The correct way to address a letter

It shows the **name** of the **person**

the **number** of the **house**

the **name** of the **road**

the **town** or **city**

the **county** and the **postcode**

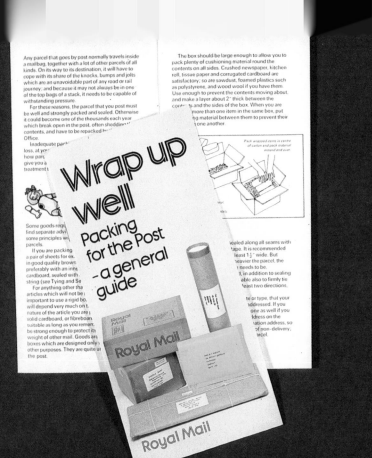

Any parcel that goes by post normally travels inside a mailbag, together with a lot of other parcels of all kinds. On its way to its destination, it will have to cope with its share of the knocks, bumps and jolts which are an unavoidable part of any road or rail journey; and because it may not always be in one of the top bags of a stack, it needs to be capable of withstanding pressure.

For these reasons, the parcel that you post must be well and strongly packed and sealed. Otherwise it could become one of the thousands each year which break open in the post, often shedding their contents, and have to be repacked by the Post Office.

Inadequate packing can result in loss, at your own expense. This shows how parcels are handled and will give you an idea of the sort of treatment that your parcel will get.

Some goods require special care. You can find separate advice on these. Here are some principles which apply to most parcels.

If you are packing something flat, say a pair of sheets for example, wrap it up in good quality brown paper, preferably with an inner wrapping of cardboard, sealed with a good quality string (see Tying and Sealing).

For anything other than flat articles which will not bend, it is important to use a rigid box. This will depend very much on the nature of the article you are packing, solid cardboard or fibreboard is suitable as long as you remember it must be strong enough to protect its contents and the weight of other mail. Goods are often sold in boxes which are designed only for display or other purposes. They are quite unsuitable for the post.

The box should be large enough to allow you to pack plenty of cushioning material round the contents on all sides. Crushed newspaper, kitchen roll, tissue paper and corrugated cardboard are satisfactory; so are sawdust, foamed plastics such as polystyrene, and wood wool if you have them. Use enough to prevent the contents moving about, and make a layer about 2" thick between the contents and the sides of the box. When you are packing more than one item in the same box, put plenty of cushioning material between them to prevent their touching one another.

Pack wrapped items in centre of carton and pack material around and over

sealed along all seams with tape. It is recommended at least 1½" wide. But the heavier the parcel, the needs to be.

in addition to sealing able also to firmly tie at least two directions.

te or type, that your addressed. If you one as well if you dress on the ation address, so of non-delivery; arcel.

Wrap up well

Packing for the Post – a general guide

Royal Mail

Royal Mail

Royal Mail

In 1784 the first mail coach ran from Bristol to London.
Twenty years afterwards there were two hundred coaches in service
with the title Royal Mail painted on their sides

Printed for & Sold by BOWLES & CARVER.

THE *ORIGINAL*
Invented by Mᵣ Palmer *of* BATH